Epicenter Press, Inc., is a regional press founded in Alaska whose interests include but are not limited to the arts, history, environment, and diverse cultures and lifestyle of the North Pacific and high latitudes. We seek both the traditional and innovative in publishing high-quality nonfiction tradebooks, contemporary art and photography giftbooks, and destination travel guides emphasizing Alaska, Washington, Oregon, and California.

The Iditarod Trail Committee holds registered trademarks for the following terms and language: Iditarod, Iditarod Trail Committee, Iditarod Trail Alaska, Alaska where men are men and women win the Iditarod, The Last Great Race, 1,049 miles, Anchorage to Nome, and Mushing the Iditarod Trail.

Editor: Kent Sturgis
Design and illustration: Amanda Brannon
Research assistant: Nancy Gates
Text ©1998 Tricia Brown
Illustrations ©1998 Amanda Brannon

Library of Congress Catalog Card Number: 98-072720
ISBN 0-945397-69-0

To order single copies of Lessons My Sled Dog Taught Me, send $9.95 (Washington residents add 86 cents state sales tax) plus $3 for priority mail shipping to: Epicenter Press, Box 82368, Kenmore, WA 98028.

Booksellers: Retail discounts are available from our trade distributor, Graphic Arts Center Publishing, Portland, Oregon; phone 800-452-3032.

Printed in Canada
First printing, August 1998
10 9 8 7 6 5 4 3 2 1

LESSONS MY SLED DOG TAUGHT ME

Humor and Heartwarming Tails
from Alaska's Mushers

Collected By Tricia Brown

Illustrations By Amanda Brannon

EPICENTER PRESS

FAIRBANKS · SEATTLE

For the dogs, who worship unworthy gods.

With my thanks to Stan Hooley, Jack Niggemyer, Joanne Potts, and Deb Walker of the Iditarod Trail Committee. Also, thanks to Bob Eley and Deborah Ryan of the Yukon Quest International Sled Dog Race for your assistance. —T.B.

CONTENTS

The Heart of a Sled Dog

My dinner partner at the pre-race Iditarod mushers' banquet was a Seattle veterinarian who'd flown up to work as a volunteer vet. In Anchorage, he'd found he couldn't just walk onto that team. There were so many volunteer vets from around the country, his name was added to a list. Disappointing, yes, but he was thrilled just to have conducted a few pre-race health checks.

"I can't believe the difference between these dogs and the couch potatoes I see back home," he said, shaking his head. Whereas the pampered pets got fat on a thousand calories a day, the sled dogs were racing-weight lean with ten or fifteen times the calories. The hearts of the athletes were well-developed, efficient muscles moving so much blood, he said, that a murmur wasn't necessarily a sign of bad health.

As I moved around the banquet room that night interviewing mushers for this book, I learned more about heart of a sled dog. The mushers spoke about hearts that remember the way to a place they've visited only once. Hearts that yearn to please, that understand their place in the team. Hearts that without knowledgeable, caring supervision will run until exhausted. The mushers also had a few good jokes to share.

In Lessons My Sled Dog Taught Me, we hear from the wise and the wise-crackers, insider jokes and touching stories from recreational mushers as well as the sprint and distance racers who enliven Alaska's favorite sport. And as you'll see, their stories about their dogs are straight from the heart.

—Tricia Brown

9

THE REWARDS

12
.

The dogs have taught me to sit back and enjoy the simple things in life.

DALTON FIEDLER, Willow
Four-time Junior Iditarod musher

14

You can never waste time sitting still and cuddling a puppy. That time comes back to you later in affection from the dog and its willingness to run for you.

DEEDEE JONROWE, Willow
Fastest woman in Iditarod history

The dogs have taught me to enjoy the outdoors.

KEN CHASE, Anvik, Alaska
Iditarod veteran

15

I finally learned there are some things more important than dogs and the Iditarod.

16
.

DAVID MILNE, Scotland
and Two Rivers, Alaska,
Introducing his date at the
'98 Iditarod mushers' banquet

A good dog musher needs a short memory. On the Iditarod, you keep asking yourself, "Why am I here?" and you think about all the work you've done over the last nine months. But it ain't but a short time before you're leaving Nome and have the next year all planned out.

LAVON BARVE, Wasilla
Yukon Quest champion, Iditarod veteran

18

I learned how to sleep comfortably. I used to sleep with my arms under my head, all curled up. Then I saw how the dogs slept stretched out. I sleep so good now.

NORA GRUNER, Fairbanks
Recreational musher

My dogs have taught me many of life's lessons about responsibility, passion, sportsmanship and respect.

DAN SEAVEY, Seward
Junior Iditarod musher
Third-generation competitor

Every aspect of my life has been enriched by the dogs. I've been mushing since I was four years old, so I have thirty-five years of appreciation for them.

MITCH SEAVEY,
Seward
Iditarod veteran

21

22
.

I learned that I don't have the patience, commitment, time, or money to race dogs.

JACK NIGGEMYER, Wasilla
Recreational musher
Iditarod Race Manager

23.

In 1989, Iditarod rookie KATHY HALVERSON of Anchorage learned that some things were more important than placing in the money. She and a handful of other mushers saved the life of another competitor when they stopped to administer first aid.

"Our hopes and dreams for Rookie of the Year were dissolved," Halverson said. "But I sleep better at night knowing that I helped . . . rather than having selfish reasons for not stopping."

The average musher has no idea how resilient dogs are. No matter how tough you think you are as a person, the dogs far exceed that. That is the key to winning races.

DICK MACKEY, Nenana
Iditarod champion

25

Take good care of them from the beginning. Spend a lot of time with them in a good, fun atmosphere. The payoff is you'll have healthy dogs.

MIKE WILLIAMS, Akiak, Alaska
Iditarod musher

This is kind of like getting a welfare check and thanking the people of America.

PADDY SANTUCCI, Tanana and Fairbanks,
reading his sponsor list for the 1998 Yukon Quest

28

If you are good to the dogs, they are good to you. They'll do all they can to help you.

JOB NOACHUCK KOKOCHURUK,
Nome elder
Mushed working dogs
on hunting trips and wood hauls

Melissa was the only dog in history that won the Iditarod, the North American, and the Anchorage Fur Rendezvous World Championship Sled Dog Race — all for Carl.

JERRY AUSTIN, St. Michael, Alaska
Describing the 1976 Iditarod team he assembled
with help from Carl Huntington's kennel

29

You could run this race twenty-five years in a row and never figure out how the dogs do it—how they run a thousand miles in ten or twelve days just because you've asked them to. I want to thank Al, Kennedy, Zack, Ranger, Rusty, Rudy, Cinder, and Zero.

TIM MOWRY, Fairbanks
Completed the Yukon Quest eight times and
the Iditarod Trail Sled Dog Race twice

When people comment that there are three generations of Seaveys racing sled dogs, I always say, "The sins of the father are perpetuated to the successive generations." It's pretty gratifying, really.

DAN SEAVEY, Seward
Ran the 1st and 25th Iditarod races

31

32

Sprint racing is extremely addictive. Worse than cocaine and just as expensive.

DORI HOLLINGSWORTH,
Seward
Sprint musher

People don't realize how athletic the dogs are. If you did an autopsy on a race dog and a wolf . . . the race dog's heart is two, three times bigger; it's lungs are two, three times bigger. They are superior athletes.

CURTIS ERHART, Fairbanks
Breeds dogs for mid-distance and Iditarod;
Competes with a sprint team

34

36
.

Watching all the energy they put forth, the dogs have taught me to be very humble. Whether it's warm, cold, 80 mph winds, they go on. They're so dedicated.

DAVID SAWATZKY, Healy, Alaska
Yukon Quest and Iditarod veteran

38

Running the Iditarod completely changed my life. It made me aware I could do anything if I put my mind to it.

JON VAN ZYLE, Chugiak, Alaska
Artist, two-time Iditarod musher

COMPLAINTS & SUGGESTIONS

42
.

My hard-earned lesson: Never turn your back on the dogs. Or they'll be long gone.

DON HONEA, Ruby, Alaska
Iditarod musher

44

Running dogs has taught me to pack food and drinks that don't freeze.

CHARLIE JORDAN, Tanana
1998 Junior Iditarod champion

It is better to stop and rest so you can go fast and have fun, than to go slow and get last place and be bummed. Fast equals fun!

TONY WILLIS, Anchorage
Junior Iditarod musher

46

Run as best you can, but enjoy the trip.

TERRY ADKINS, Sand Coulee, Montana
Competed in the Iditarod 21 times

48

Don't second-guess your leader, especially in bad weather.

RAMEY SMYTH, Big Lake, Alaska
Two-time Junior Iditarod champion, Iditarod musher

   Keep your guard up, says sprint racer NITA HOLLINGSWORTH, even when you believe the worst part of the trail is behind you. In the 1994 Junior World Championship, the Seward musher had safely taken several treacherous corners at high speeds. She cracked up when she least expected to — on a straightaway.

   "I hit a stump sticking up out of the snow. My sled shot into the air, and so did I. I woke up lying in the snow with a busted sled, busted arm, and no dogs."

50

My dogs have taught me that it is better to go slow than not go at all! Baby steps . . . baby steps . . .

JIM GALLEA, Seeley Lake, Montana,
Junior Iditarod musher

Never overrun 'em because then they won't eat.

RAYMIE REDINGTON, Knik, Alaska
Iditarod musher

51

52.

Train! If I don't train them well enough, I have to run up the hills. And I've done a lot of that! I lost twenty pounds on the 1998 race.

STEVE ADKINS,
Trapper Creek, Alaska
Iditarod musher

If they ain't got no one for them to follow, they won't go.

MICHAEL KING, Salcha, Alaska,
who scratched from the 1998 Yukon Quest
with a young dog in lead

53

54

Have faith in your team.

ANDY WILLIS, Anchorage
Iditarod musher

A lot of people base too much on their first impression of a dog. The first impression isn't necessarily going to be accurate. A little bit shy doesn't mean the dog doesn't have a strong head. A dog that shows early promise as a leader may not have his head together.

PETER BUTTERI, Tok, Alaska
Completed the Yukon Quest six times

55

"Last year I was real sick and my dogs were happy," said 1998 Yukon Quest musher LARRY CARROLL. "They kept looking back at me and saying, 'Poor son-of-a-gun.' This year I felt good and my dogs were sick."

Traveling with a sick dog in the sled bag, Carroll suddenly heard a strange sound. He stopped, unzipped the bag, and discovered that the dog had thrown up on everything ("My boots, my hat, the cooler . . . ") After cleaning up the mess, Carroll said, "I didn't feel so bad for him, so I let him run. I didn't figure he wasn't that sick anymore."

The moral of the story: Don't put a sick dog in the bag until after he's puked.

**Watch your mouth.
Dogs and small children
might be listening.**

ANONYMOUS

58

Mushers like to think of themselves as more important than they are. Humans are but one factor in the training program. The dogs teach each other more than the humans do.

JOHN WOOD,
Anchorage
Sprint musher

59

The main thing is to have a good time. If you don't have a good time, you're in trouble because you can't always succeed in your goals.

JACQUES PHILIP, Willow, Alaska, and France
Distance musher in Alaska and Europe

In the old days, the dog care was different, the food was different. Feed your dogs dried fish and beaver and they went all right.

RUDY DEMOSKI, Wasilla
Veteran sprint and
distance musher

60

I've never been involved in a sport that will take you through so many different emotions in such a short time. You can be going along on a beautiful run, on a great day, and your dogs running well, thinking 'This is a great team.' And you round a corner and things suddenly go haywire — it can happen so quickly!

KELI MAHONEY, Talkeetna, Alaska
Ran her second Iditarod in 1998

61
.

TRUSTING HEARTS

I accept this award on behalf of all the mushers still on the trail, in the middle of the night, far from the checkpoint, on their hands and knees, taking care of their dogs. Nobody's talking, nobody's sleeping, nobody's eating. They're moving up and down the line of dogs, taking care of little aches and pains.

DAVE OLESEN, Great Slave Lake, Canada
Winner, Alyeska Vet's Choice Award,
1998 Yukon Quest

66

"Thank God Charlie's got the right trail," CHRISTOPHER KNOTT thought as his lead dog finally spied a trail marker through a swirling snowstorm along the Bering Sea. For a while, the 1998 Iditarod musher had no idea where he was headed. After three hours of creeping along, Knott's leaders, Hotfoot and Charlie, suddenly stopped.

"What's going on?!" Knott wondered. The snow was blowing so hard, he could barely see past the end of his sled, let alone to his leaders. He set his ice hook and struggled to the front of the team. There he discovered Charlie standing on the very steps of the checkpoint.

"I have no idea why he went to that building. He'd never been there before," Knott said.

If you've got a good connection with your dogs, you're a part of them and they're a part of you. They're an extension of your arm. If you feel from down deep, those dogs will feel it. We all focus as one mind.

JOE GARNIE, Teller, Alaska
Iditarod veteran

67

Dogs teach you what unconditional love is all about.

JACK BERRY, Homer, Alaska,
who married his wife on the frozen Bering Sea
at Nome following his 1998 Iditarod finish.

The sled dog is your friend. You train them. And they're athletes. But you've got to be friends with them. There has to be trust. If they don't trust you, they're not going to give you what you need to be a winner.

SHANNON ERHART, Fairbanks
Breeds middle-distance and Iditarod dogs;
competes on sprint circuit

69

RICK MACKEY's 1998 Yukon Quest leader, Cindy, was taking the team through Fortymile country in her second Quest when she approached a closed-up cabin that had been a checkpoint a year earlier. There were no markers or broken trail. And yet the young dog remembered the place and tried to pull in. That taught Mackey this:

"Trust your leaders and you'll stay out of trouble. They know where they're going . . . or at least where they went last year!"

From running dogs I've learned how the different parts of a team work together. You've got lead dogs, wheel dogs, swing dogs, and team dogs, and they all have to fulfill their particular function for the team to do well. Just like in life, we all have our part.

DARYL HOLLINGSWORTH, Seward
Sprint racer

71

Your dogs are always right. The dogs never make mistakes. When we try to make them do something they've never been taught, we make mistakes.

HOWARD FARLEY, Nome
Helped organize the first Iditarod in 1973,
co-founded the new Nome Kennel Club in 1974

What I love about sled dogs is they trust you to make their decisions for them. And if you make mistakes, they still love you.

GERRI HANSCHEN, Seward
Sprint musher

73

74
.

Dogs like consistent behavior throughout training and racing. If you suddenly pull something out of the hat and make a change, that would break the trust.

MATT HAYASHIDA, Big Lake, Alaska
Iditarod musher

Having sled dogs is like having kids. It changes your life. Like children, they need daily, if not constant, attention.

JIM LANIER, Chugiak
Iditarod musher

76

WHY THEY CALL IT DOGGED PERSUIT

80

I've got to win. That would be the turning point in a guy's career, to win the Iditarod. Everything would go well after that.

TIM OSMAR, Clam Gulch, Alaska
Three-time Junior Iditarod champion,
Copper Basin 300 champion,
Yukon Quest musher, Iditarod veteran

81
.

82

The dogs are happiest when they have a job to do. You treat them right and give them a fair chance and they're just amazing.

LIBBY RIDDLES, Wasilla
First woman to win the Iditarod, 1985

If you get to a point where you don't feel you can make any improvements, then you're going to be going downhill, because there's somebody out there who's making improvements.

RICK SWENSON, Two Rivers, Alaska
Five-time Iditarod champion

A lot of people who are good in the race will succeed in other fields. They want to be perfect. They do the best they can. Maybe they won't win, but they will be at a high level, always performing.

CLAIRE PHILIP,
Willow, Alaska, and France
Distance musher in
Alaska and Europe

85
.

I've learned how to keep my balance when I'm sleeping and how to hang on tight! (I drag pretty well.)

JENNIFER DEYE, Cambridge, Minnesota
Junior Iditarod musher

My dogs have taught me patience ... strength ... skill ... and determination. That's what it takes to get to Nome.

SONNY KING,
Spartanburg, South Carolina,
Veterinarian,
ran his second Iditarod in 1998

88

BILL BASS tells this story illustrating the durability of his dogs during a "five-dog night":

"In the Iditarod in '92, I got stuck out in my sleeping bag with five dogs on top of me. There was a fifty- or sixty-knot wind, and the chill was seventy below. I had a little radio and I heard they were looking for us."

Within hours, rescuers found Bass and his team.

"There were five teams within fifty yards of each other and we didn't know each other was there. It was absolutely amazing."

89

90

Solo is our kennel mascot. He's old now, but in his day, he was a main leader. He wasn't the fastest, but he was always able to get up and go. He taught me that when things get tough, that's more important.

LINWOOD FIEDLER, Willow
Iditarod musher

MARY SHIELDS of Salcha, Alaska, learned about perseverance from running dogs. She and Lolly Medley were groundbreakers when they ran the Iditarod in 1974. That was the second year of the race, but the first year for women to enter—and finish.

"At the starting line, someone hollered, 'You better turn around now, you'll never make it,' " Shields recalled. "That meant for sure I was going to."

We're a pack and I'm the alpha male. No more, no less. They do their part, I do my part, and we're a team.

92
.

CHARLIE BOULDING, Manley, Alaska
Two-time Yukon Quest champion,
Kuskokwim 300 champion,
Kobuk 440 champion,
Iditarod veteran

I've learned over the years that the dogs are smarter than humans when it comes to communication. They know what you're thinking at all times.

GEORGE ATTLA, North Pole
Champion sprint musher
Iditarod musher

98

Believe and you will achieve.

JEFF KING, Denali Park,
Three-time Iditarod champion,
Yukon Quest champion,
Three-time Kuskokwim 300 champion,
Coldfoot Classic champion

Anytime I'm under stress, I try to get to where the dogs are mentally — they don't care where Rick Swenson is or where Doug Swingley is. They just care about being with me.

VERN HALTER,
Trapper Creek, Alaska
Two-time Yukon
 Quest champion,
Iditarod veteran

Some dogs have to learn the hard way.

Iditarod musher JOHN BARRON found this out the year his leader, Oogruk, was headed toward a hole in the ice. Barron gave Oogruk a "Gee" to go right.

"He didn't take the gee, and he slipped into the hole," Barron remembers. The river current was so strong that the dog was being pushed under the ice and its harness was slipping off. With his heart pounding, Barron flipped his sled on its side and hurried forward. He reached in, grabbed a handful of skin and harness, and pulled Oogruk to safety.

"After that, when I said 'Gee,' when I said 'Haw,' he was right there!"

You don't realize what it takes in time and commitment to run. It's like any professional sport. The mental side is just as big as doing the Super Bowl.

ZACK STEER, Anchorage
1998 Iditarod rookie

When you're out on the trail and you make a decision to stop for a certain amount of time, stick with that decision. In the checkpoints, it's easy to get excited and change your mind. In mushing, like most other things, your first choice is generally your best.

104

TED ENGLISH, Willow
Iditarod musher

When you're tired or bummed out, the dogs bring you out of it. The things we worry about, they just don't give a hoot about.

RAMY BROOKS,
Fairbanks,
Iditarod musher

105
.

Sometimes they fool me.

HERBIE NAYOKPUK,
Shishmaref, Alaska
Iditarod veteran known
as "The Shishmaref
Cannonball"

106

It was the worst year you could have finished second—behind the first woman to win it.

DEWEY HALVERSON, Anchorage
Second to Libby Riddles in the 1985 Iditarod

A lot of people make the mistake of thinking dogs are human because they relate to their emotional characteristics. Dogs can be happy, sad, excited, or bored, but they live in the moment.

LYNDA PLETTNER, Big Lake
Iditarod musher

110

I had to learn from the worst dogs available. Everybody in the village of Kokhanok gave me their garbage. That probably taught me more about sled-dogging than anything.

MIKE WETHERBEE, Kasilof, Alaska
Recreational musher

It's like a coach on a ball team. You've got to put the players in the right positions, work with them, get the most out of what you've got to work with. It's a challenge to put all these individuals together and make a competitive team.

JOEE REDINGTON, JR., Knik, Alaska
Sprint and distance musher

111.

The dogs have taught me how easy it is to communicate with them, in all ways.

BOB HICKEL, Anchorage
Distance and mid-distance musher

Austrian-Canadian musher HANS GATT raced borrowed dogs one year in the Open North American Sled Dog Race in Fairbanks. The musher who loaned them advised Gatt that the dogs were whip-trained. (While the whip never really touches the dogs, they respond to the cracking sound overhead.)

"We were about three miles from the line and I cracked the whip," Gatt said. "And both of the leaders laid down."

Turns out the owner had whip-trained them to help break up dogfights. Lying down was exactly what they were supposed to do. Gatt laughed about later, even though, he said, "it cost me a couple of places in the race."

My motto with my dogs is, 'It's a great day to be alive.'

BILL SNODGRASS, Dubois, Wyoming,
Iditarod rookie in 1998

116

The dogs have as much pride as any human athlete. That's why Granite was a wonderful dog. He knew when he won. He thought he deserved all the accolades, he expected them. He was a ham in front of the media.

SUSAN BUTCHER, Fairbanks
Four-time Iditarod champion

118

They know your innermost thoughts. My old lead dog Pal knew more about me than I knew about him.

ROY MONK, Lancashire, England
Iditarod musher

120

My dogs taught me to shut up and let them do their job. On one run, I talked to my leader Socks the whole time, and finally he laid down and wouldn't get up until I shut up.

KIMARIE HANSON, Anchorage
Raced in the 1998 Iditarod
at age 18

They're working dogs, but they know when it's a race day. On working days, they're way more calm. Before a race, they bark and go wild.

CLEMENT NELSON, Kotzebue, Alaska
17-year-old sprint musher who
uses dogs to hunt, haul wood,
set up summer camp

122

When we said 'Mush!' the dogs turned around and got up on the sled, wagging their tails and wanting to be petted.

NORMAN VAUGHAN, Anchorage
Life-long adventurer who was
12 in 1917, when he first
harnessed a German shepherd
and a collie.

No two dogs are alike. That's the biggest challenge of running dogs.

AMY WRIGHT, Tok, Alaska
Yukon Quest musher,
Sprint musher

123

HARRY CALDWELL of Wasilla remembers the visions he had on the Iditarod Trail one year. Hallucinating from sleep-deprivation, Caldwell believed he was running his dogs through downtown Chicago. He saw traffic lights, signs to Wrigley Field, and people on the sidewalks waving and pointing: "Look, a dog team!" What did he gain from the experience?

"I learned to get more sleep."

126

It's just like the old-timers say. If you make one little mistake, it can lead to a bigger mistake and a bigger mistake. You always keep that in mind—don't let this thing get out of control.

JOE RUNYAN, Nenana, Alaska
Iditarod and Yukon Quest champion

As you get older, you get a little smarter.

JOE REDINGTON, SR., Knik, Alaska
Father of the Iditarod,
completed the 25th Iditarod
 at age 80

127

TRAIL MIX

Wit & Wisdom

130

I started with five adults, five pups, one three-legged dog, one borrowed dog, and a coyote. They were moving so slow, by the finish the puppies had grown up.

JOHN SCHANDELMEIER, Paxson, Alaska
Yukon Quest musher

If you want to make your dreams come true, you must stay awake.

KEITH KIRKVOLD, Fairbanks
Yukon Quest musher

133

If you run a tenth-place team like a tenth-place team, you may finish fifth. But if you run a tenth-place team like a fifth-place team, you won't finish.

DOUG HARRIS, Whitehorse, Yukon Territory
Yukon Quest musher

A dog musher needs two things: a wife and a truck. And they both have to work.

ANONYMOUS
(Conveniently so.)

135

136

The view never changes unless you're the lead dog.

ANONYMOUS

Mushing dogs is a game of feet. You really learn how important it is to take care of the dogs' feet.

MARK WEBER, Anchorage
Former Dillingham
competitive musher

137
.

138

A dog team is like a chain saw. It runs the best right before it runs out of gas.

JEROME LONGO, Willow
Iditarod musher

The harder I work, the luckier I get.

MARTIN BUSER, Big Lake, Alaska,
Three-time Iditarod champion,
Kusko 300 champion

140

In the Spring, the yard is all mud, and the dogs are muddy and pitiful-looking. They jump around and sling wet stuff across your face, and you worry about what's mixed in with the mud. Then Summer comes and the yard gets dusty. To cut down on the dust you spray the yard with water, and the mud comes back. The best part is in the Fall, as you wait for snow and get all the equipment ready to go. You look forward to that first run.

STEVE IHDE, Anchorage
Recreational musher

142

It doesn't matter who the best lead dog is — we know he's going to make the team. We need to focus on the weakest member of our organization.

MARTIN BUSER, Big Lake, Alaska,
Three-time Iditarod champion,
Kusko 300 champion

144

My wife has already committed me to next year . . . she enjoyed the vacation.

Overheard at the 1998 Yukon Quest
Finishers' Banquet in Fairbanks

146

Trust the dogs.

PAUL GEBHARDT, Kasilof
Tustumena 200 champion,
Iditarod veteran

Sled dogs have taught me to have a big checkbook.

DOUG SWINGLEY, Simms, Montana
Iditarod champion

147

148

Never eat orange slices with the same gloves you wear to feed the dogs their fish snacks.

LINDA JOY, Willow
Iditarod musher

150
.

    Never set your expectations too high if you're a rookie in a long-distance race. You'll be humbled quickly.

BRENDA MACKEY, Nenana, Alaska
1998 Yukon Quest rookie
Third-generation distance racer

A good dog can teach your team more than you could ever teach your team.

ROB CARSS, Alberta, Canada,
Iditarod rookie in 1996

152

My dogs have taught me to not interrupt them when they're busy running.

CINDY GALLEA, Seeley Lake, Montana
Iditarod rookie in 1998

154

Here's how JIM LANIER, a distance musher from Chugiak, learned that when all is said and done, dogs will be dogs:

"One real 'lowlight' of my mushing experience is when I was taking my team on a training run, and the entire team, one by one, ran through a small door and into a chicken coop. Each dog came out with a squawking chicken in its mouth."

155
.

156

From running dogs I've gotten independence and a whole new outlook on life. Also I've learned that Dingdongs are the best on the trail . . . and Twinkies don't freeze.

LINDSEY HANSON, Anchorage
Junior Iditarod musher

PHOTO: LIN MITCHELL

158

TRICIA BROWN is no dog musher, but she's seen miles of back-country from the so-called comfort of the basket (in the bottom of the sled, where tired or sick dogs ride). Brown shares her Anchorage home with a ten-year-old Golden Retriever, who has an abiding fear of dog booties, and a geriatric mutt who runs only in his sleep. An avid fan of mushing, Brown edited *Iditarod Silver: 25 Years of the Last Great Race.* She is the author of *Iditarod Country: Exploring the Route of the Last Great Race* and as this book went to press was editing a new edition of *The Alaska Almanac*®.

FASHION MEANS YOUR FUR HAT IS DEAD

**A hilarious look at manners
and social survival in Alaska.
by Mike Doogan
$14.95, paperback**

HOW TO SPEAK ALASKAN

**edited by Mike Doogan
Learn to speak Alaskan with these irreverent and witty
yet factual explanations of Alaskan's unique vocabulary.
$4.95, paperback**

**To order these books, send a check for the purchase price
(plus 8.2% sales tax on orders from Washington state) plus
$3 for postage and handling to: Epicenter Press, Box 82368,
Kenmore, WA 98028, or phone our toll-free order line at
800-950-6663. Visa/MC accepted.**